ARCADE

ARCADE

Erica Hunt
POEMS

Alison Saar
DRAWINGS

KELSEY ST. PRESS

Grateful acknowledgment is made to readers and audiences who heard early drafts of the work in this book in reading series at the St. Mark's Poetry Project, the Ear Inn, Dark Room Collective, Detroit Institute of Art, State University of New York at Buffalo Poetics Program, Naropa Institute, San Francisco State University and New Langton Arts.

"Coronary Artist" appeared in somewhat altered form in *Local History* (Roof Books 1993)

The author wishes to express her thanks to Marty Ehrlich and Madeleine Hunt-Ehrlich for their care, Alta Starr for her friendship and close readings, to the Fund for Poetry for the gift of time, and to Patricia Dienstfrey, Rena Rosenwasser and Kathleen Fraser for their support of this book.

Publication of this book was made possible by grants from the California Arts Council and the LEF Foundation.

Generous donations were also provided by:
Carole Berg, Diane Middlebrook, Denise L. Beirnes and Sandra J. Springs.

First Edition

Copyright © 1996 Erica Hunt and Alison Saar

Library of Congress Cataloging-in-Publication Data

Hunt, Erica, 1955–
    Arcade / Erica Hunt, poems; Alison Saar, drawings.
      p.   cm.
    ISBN 0-932716-39-3 (alk. paper). — ISBN 0-932716-40-7
      (alk. paper) [Limited edition, signed, with original woodcut]
    I. Saar, Alison. II. Title.
PS3558.U46766A89   1996
811'.54–dc20   96–11655
                                                                  CIP

Book design: Poulson/Gluck

Kelsey St. Press, 2718 Ninth Street, Berkeley, CA 94710
Tel. (510) 845-2260   Fax (510) 548-9185
email: kelseyst@sirius.com   web: http://www.sirius.~kelseyst/welcome.html

Kelsey St. Press books are distributed by:
Small Press Distribution: Tel. (800) 869-7553   (510) 549-3336   Fax (510) 549-2201
Bookpeople: Tel. (800) 999-4650   (510) 632-4700   Fax (510) 632-1281

in memoriam
Jerry Estrin

and to the future,
Maddy, Julian & Kyle

Contents

First Words — 9

Coronary Artist — 13

Magritte's Black Flag — 18

Starting with A — 19

Motion Sickness — 21

Squeeze Play — 25

Arcade — 26

the voice of no — 28

Science of the Concrete — 30

Focus — 33

Fortune — 34

Personal — 35

Madame Narcissist — 37

so sex, the throne whose abrasions we crave — 40

after Baudelaire's "The Muse for Hire" — 41

Risk Signature — 43

Biographical Suite — 46

Variation — 50

COLLABORATIVE STATEMENT — 53

First Words

Night exits fast
to the sky painted
huge ahead of itself
the morning appears
an alien character
mauve on the set
where I am the Sunday
company
glad to be a passenger
slumped
on a wobbling planet
tilted in risen dawn.

I stray from my lines
my mind
a moving target
Stand
speaking to the sky
even if its lights are punched out
Night falling into dawn
the shadows change
what's under stones or understates
the tension of what's concealed
and what's shown.

Awake nude to match reality
where words fill the future
with mental muscle
and facts ripen into the clauses
waiting for them —

awake
nude to grief whose
unstuck clatter rises
above the mutter of corpses

awake, just as I am
ready to sit by my relic
and make it work
prepared to rot
with the last
vestiges of meaning
the words won't write themselves
out of their depth unless someone
listens to them

the words in books no one reads
are already unwriting themselves

the words that return in the face
the face of the familiar
defend the overwritten

the words at the center
or at a dead end
use grammar to parse their decease

the words that unbutton the
pants of ardent description

the words leading from one thing to the next
shift as you enter

the words in bones
stand for what they are part of

the words that overstate
hyperbolize

the words that give nothing
beyond the marks carried in ourselves
ensure we don't spill a drop

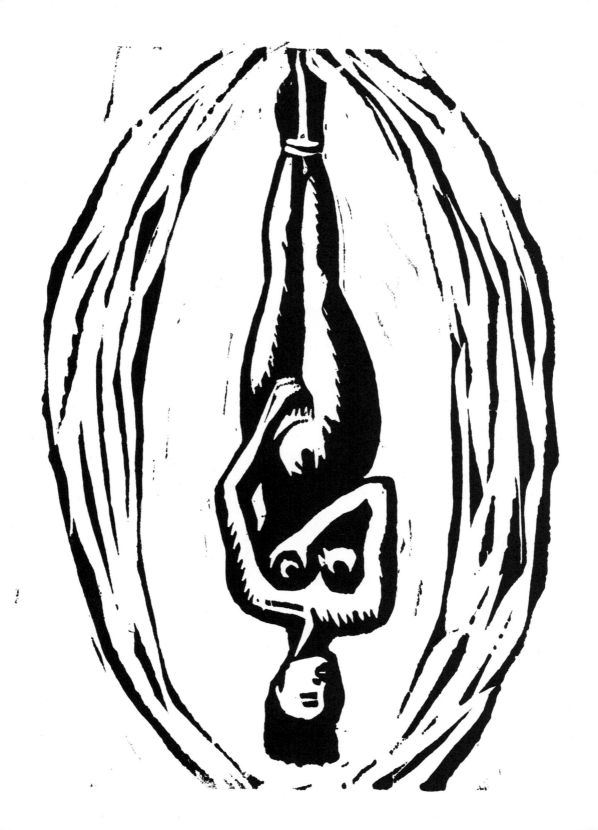

Coronary Artist (1)

I dream excess — high-speed vision. Snow falling upwards. The bed in a corner of the empty lot. Cut logs careening away from the saw. They know what's waiting for them. A line of introduction. Incomplete arc of contemplation. A family of clothes begging to be picked up. Chimneys at work carrying steam. Ingest coffee, loosen stuck bits of unvoiced flux loved for their silence.

All the great heroes slept late. The common folks get up early and fight for the victory. It takes a lifetime to be steered in this direction; snow is mounting from the sky down. I think the dirty clothes are crying and want to be washed. Piles of clothes begin to mount from the sky down. I would say no, except for the empty chair where taking off is perfected.

The left brain turns the other cheek. The right brain can't imagine it. To be bringing one's face into morning when it is barely light. To promote sunshine to my daughter while surviving my own ferocious will to sleep. This is the corner to turn to the bathroom. This is the sink. I look at myself in the mirror and see the person I might have been had I gotten more sleep. I step back into the world, it is warmer and moister than I thought. It is a whole world, with its own affections, anxieties, welcome.

Custom has it that a woman gets up first to solve the dilemma of the burning moment.

You can smell the smoke answering the alarm. And then you can't smell anything over the family sound track, putting everything on hold. One becomes an adult without knowing the details of how it was done, only knowing which team you're on, which hat corresponds to your glands. Already this is an extinct culture, a culture of giants prone to the vertigo of silent agreements and unenforceable contracts. The rocks in our beds belong to them. Their sexual politics get the better of us sometimes and we are left with dream transcriptions and delinquencies instead of passion outside the parentheses.

We make it to the crossroads only to come to a total stop. The idea we harbor is subversive. That there may be many moments in which we recognize the sources of our hunger, falling out of the sky, a complete thought in the center of our most visible selves.

Coronary Artist (2)

Though what I live now is ordinary, I have lived through the glory of numbers. I have visited zero in the sense of absolute beginning to watch fate bleed uncontrollably through a vast chain of explanatory footnotes wound like a bandage over the simplest matter.

I have resisted the power of spelling and broken the spell of pronouns inventing continuity where persons and personalities change sides. I have peered through a keyhole into that narrow room, history, where it is happening to someone else upstairs overhead wearing heavy shoes.

Pathetic, awkward, overdoing it, thumping around breaking into static, fend off the eros to which we react, never initiate, grabbing instead what stales our everyday, our faded monotony. Who wouldn't kick in their sleep and wander off the path of managed impulse? Who wouldn't aspire to become an alien in their own language for a moment to lose the feeling of being both separated and crowded by their experience?

The flowers wear pink as if coming down with the fever. The first to let go were the attributes losing hold of their objects. I was there on my tippy toes feeling thickness leave me, my palms turning into asterisks, my bent arms into commas.

A little display of excitement waved, produced in me the memory of companionship. I watched myself follow the wave and disappear over the crest of a hill in a stuttering laugh.

My back bristled with the urge to give chase, to demand a say, to reconfigure paradise with perfect weather and regular elections. But the distances confused me. Where I stand now, I shout out of my body armor. I whisper parts of the roar.

Coronary Artist (3)

In a dream I go to a room of spare parts.
We apply porcelain to our hair.
There are special scholars who study temples.
Someone sweeps shoulder-length tresses across the floor.
Arms in varieties of salute beckon, bent and dimpled.
I have one leg up.
I'm not fast enough and they take the other.
They hand me costume lips.
My ears are festooned.
What remains after my waist is whittled is little more
    than a functioning crease.
I bat my eyes to practice fascination.
But of particular concern is my hair, my hair, my hair.
So dry it crackles, as it is french-twisted and lacquered bright vermillion.
With this hair I stop traffic, eliminate the inconvenience of passageways,
duration between significant events, for something is always happening,
I travel through mirrors, I'm on the subway platform and the train comes,
an IND. I get on.

Magritte's Black Flag

There will be delays this morning on the Number 4 express train to Woodlawn. Express passengers are advised to wait for the Number 5 or 6 running on the local track.

The Number 6 local will also be delayed this morning due to unusually high volume on the local track. Delays are expected through the morning.

Passengers are advised to take alternate routes to their destination, such as the N or R lines. The N & R lines have been switched to the LL tracks to make room for additional 5 & 6 trains making all BMT stops.

The LL trains have been moved to the Number 1 line. The Number 1 is on the 2 and the 2 is on the Three.

The Number 7 has been suspended this morning. To get to Queens, please go upstairs and get a transfer for the shuttle bus to the F train which is providing temporary service to Queens Plaza.

Passengers traveling to Long Island City must complete their travel by 7 P.M. tonight when all service to Long Island City will be discontinued. Passengers wishing to continue to Long Island City are advised that there are buses at the 59th Street Bridge. Bus schedules have not yet been made public.

Starting with A

She passes through pockets of warm air in a cold season, assailed by night noises, sounds in a correspondence based more on bravura than the contents of this failing world.

Start with A as in ANT, and give to every terror a soothing name.

Death is a white boy backing out a lawnmower from the garage, staring down the black girl's hello, silently re-entering the cool shell of his house.

Is it an accident? She is working without quotes, never looking down.

The sunlight thickens at the end of the day bringing the edges of things nearer, sharp laughs that break the honeyed silences.

In night country all routes are approximately marked. There the exact temperature of the prison can be felt, the degrees distancing "home" from its public relations and denial. At night the shortest moments rustle in their chains; the invisible blends in.

Motion Sickness

Go
direct to dare
lift a finger
to the head
into transparency
spot
vanishing detail
accelerate to
simplify notes
industrial strength
fresh air
pours in the brain
arranged to fit
the stories plus
new slogans.

The round trip
supplies the proof
of a last word
tune
tin tongue
ritual
spoon
spin spun
pinned on
words

Walked around
in the stopped clock
present
wondering which
apparently random
twitch is worse
which right is worn
out, which one
to win back
to a short leash
or lash
or limit
minus the imagination
minus the concrete
minus the fuck
minus the pause
minus the minus
emptying the empty
except denser

To be sure snacks kill the appetite.
The feeling of drama kills the feeling of action.
The feeling of the surreal sells perfume.

Brink or break
flight's forward
forth into it
intuit
as in
overdo it
overtaking
the fifth
can't help it,
can't help listening
as in incriminating
myself
can't help this

stirring, striking
jumping,
to disrupt
the correct slant
in the walls
created by pictures
the buttons sticky with
manipulated bring-backs
ray charles instead of
face to face talk
erase talk

race talk
erases race
chases thought
down disowned
alleys of envied
sports figures
divides eros from
commotion where
narcissus sits
cooling his heels

the corridor awaits
leading out of control
over the bridge made of
common sense, the
figure in the words.

Squeeze Play

The bloom falls off this week's celestial. First act tragedy, the second act a second guess, a second wind blowing through the endless reign of disconnected singularities…

Say, again?

Ascetic demi-caesuras pick over the game, squeeze the comma and duck the consequence. Stuck behind the letters of the law, they miss the spirit.

What?

A habit is a permanent accident. Invisible this — hairs split or lost on the way to the prize, the unintentional speck or word or bird deflects fact, raises flaw to the level of tactics.

Mood swings this way and that. By turns garrulous or retiring. Our habits keep a firm tug on the dramatis personae: weight lifter, head shrinker, starlet, prison warden, escape artist, resolutely chained to their own paragraphs with a list of predictable desires.

The culture beats the brow with equal parts spectacle and punishment, often in the same sitcom (coming to a theater *in you*), all the repeats we've seen before. The middle class crashes, the dreams of the people fade, the heroine is a figure made of glass at which we each get a turn to throw our voices, choose the answer, the witnesses and the weapons, our most intimate proofs.

Arcade

Blistering routine, I muse through events until I'm in deep, so deep, I no longer notice the D or the P, the down down dirty dirt, the relative positions, who's behind the barbwire and who's in front, within and without, gagged angels of liberalism burying the hatchet in the social body, leaving it for dead.

I don't notice the clock, cartwheeling its way to the end of the millennium, the fix in the race, nor the tick in platonic bombs beneath the feet of an undecided public standing on a ledge.

Anymore.

I swim in this lack, swimmer in a salty non-solution, current events on one side, the present on the other, running neck and neck. Non-events sell newspapers but are curiously unreported, not even as consolation for the tense freedoms we don't miss.

Each day salved by a dozen analgesics applied to my sore spots, from my hemorrhoids to my teeth set on edge, I travel to the "World of Work!"™ to face down the day to day until one of us surrenders. I go for bonus points by being closest to the train door when it enters the station. But the mood wears off and I can smell the stench of the anesthetic sting my nose as I begin the count backwards into a childhood powerlessness, a childhood where authority defers to your wishes to the point of forgetting about them.

I want to pull a tantrum, the emergency cord, slam on the brakes of this moving forward which is really a standing still at the station. The conductor comes on the intercom and intones an explanation as if he were the narrator and I were the ghost in unrelated and overlapping plots.

We wait in the dark. We cannot tell if we are at the brink again or just in the middle. Are we on an incline or are we stranded, far away from any suitable destination?

We try to scan the headlines at a polite distance. Of course no one believes a word of what we know will be written there, even when they throw the predictable live bait before the blood-bored crowds. We wear our indifference with dignity, in fact, it gives us dignity, separates us from those who've been taken in or begun to fade in the glare of the bright arcade lights, the rings and buzzes — crowding those who live the war game instead of play it, just past the point where a thought can be followed.

Coda

Against the complete dark, against bureaucratic seizures of the possible, against the body buckling itself against the irregularities of desire, the multiplication of parallel lines meet over the fold in the mind, just past the point where a thought can be followed, where the curve is constant, motion displacing motion, checkers in black spaces and fluctuating light...

the voice of no

No need to be contrary, I put on a face.
No use for muscle, the workers stand on line for hours.
No need to read, 24 hours of the shopping channel.
No fire, we have the illusion of doing what we want.

Is that any way to talk with your tongue pressed against glass?
The tv set is barking this Sunday morning off
when we acquire an instant memory,
and round language, where the ends justify the ends.
We rummage among the many
unplugged connections

looking for that darn
fraction of a percent of the landscape
you say it is possible to live in,
who will miss
it when we divide up
the sun, devour the
young rather than
give up our good seats.
The postcards
are bought out,
the lp is skipping
and anyway
rescue is sure to be slow.
In place of a raft
we paddle
ladders past the
litter of drifting bodies.

Science of the Concrete

At first you see
only its description
the skin
a container of its
umber
its beauty
folded into the carved
surface
then you don't know
what you are seeing
whether it is the object
you see or the shadow
you see
falling
completely before
the body stops
falling
in its dream
that hangs
there.

and when it is done
the statue appears
as a couple
still sitting
there never
breaking
an embrace in
one piece.

II

its "back" away from you
so you "know" which way
to face, and with what
attitude
in the language of backs
to regard as complete
whether ambidextrous or not
whether we exaggerate
the numbers of sides
or smooth the planes
of slow shifting hips.

the unseen part
is a controlling force
over bodies written off
as repetition of the already seen
degrees of sex
and color
to be held against
backed
against
the wall
and halved
unrecognizably
halved.

people "make"
the people around them
and they write
to write
the reader
out of retreat,
out of distant austerity
concealing this same
fragile activity
people make
each other
part by part
then whole
into *whole*.

Focus

Merchandising mines culture quagmire for transparent glory.

Lucid limits of an elegant friction.

Irrational transfer of the last cuticle crumb.

The warrior tickets are always stamped for the food table.

The meat looks like it belongs in a circus.

The kindness of months replaces spirit of unlimited demand for sacrifice, so that men in business suits may grow fat.

One "I" too many betrays the just balances.

Whistle and the jury stands up.

The witnesses rise out of a pumpkin.

Looking for a trope to serve us/ save us.

The burning house is an apt metaphor.

The sensation of oxygen removed.

Fortune

We haven't entered enough contests and won. But we'll correct that — we'll break the bank and go from one to the other, sweepstakes winners, lotto lovers, zero demons, a terrible crew of arrivistes, swilling seltzer and ordering books they don't have in the kitchen. Watch out. We will leave a winning streak in our wake, like the sign of Zorro, like a hunter with her ear to the ground, looking for the next roll of dice, like a window you can see *through*.

Go ahead, make some noise. This morning lives for racket, it makes the sun rise faster, part fact, part fiction. We wake up to make ends meet — to make ends meet.

Personal

Logic seeks object to undergo rigorous eye witness;
the rest a test of patience.
Objects collected: cloak of visibility,
hypothetical continuity,
simultaneously independent propositions;
grammar — a cause.
No reasonable emotion refused.

Madame Narcissist

I have the power of simultaneous affect; it breaks off in a smile.

I adore the arbitrary embrace of *you.*

I light up the reader.

Even my dark side is worthy of study.

Every day my pennies turn a thought.

I see my ideas everywhere, on the brink of worldwide acceptance and potential profit.

I believe my silence speaks volumes.

I have as many layers as any serial killer.

I'm in the moment.

I play that game when I'm bored.

I believe the story about the father who drove to work and left his child in back in the carseat all day.

I believe in personal contact.

Nothing escapes my notice.

Everything around me is subject to decay.

I've lost count.

I teach these kids more than they need to know.

I have the same number of stitches.

I don't know how it happened, I was just standing here.

I know they are after me.

I know the author.

I already have a better angle on this.

I do not go out of my way so I am never out of the picture.

II

I am sentenced to think in lines running away and toward radical detachment, where "I"s lock.

A tractor song imitating life (art) running down the rows, I think, of selective flamboyance.

Phone calls preempt the buzzless space around me.

The trail gives out; vines cover it.

I sweep up the impulses of intangible dread, along with the prior generations' conviction that the rules of destiny entail implacable random betrayal, where no good deed goes unpunished. Others are mourning dead ironies. Which end is related?

I seek legibility.

I read clouds; continental doubt.

I tend to color the facts, unbinding private property so it multiplies.

I hold on to time; I summon the past. Still my gaze simulates connection.

In sleep the brain wills it, my fingers pick out the thread.

so sex, the throne whose abrasions we crave

today or tomorrow I will shove the books off my bed
and pick up my lap and go somewhere where I have longed to go.

I will make myself narrow and let another body pass through.
I will let go of the wheel for a moment.

Sing road hymns over the bumps.
Chat over the table feeling the heat rise.

I will let the odd curve merge.
I will be the first to touch.

I will be the touch, before it is dry.

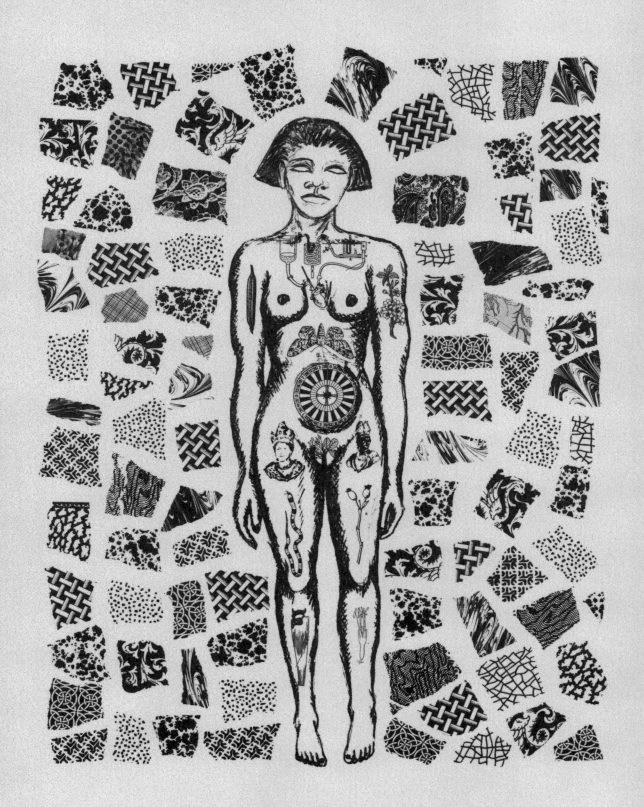

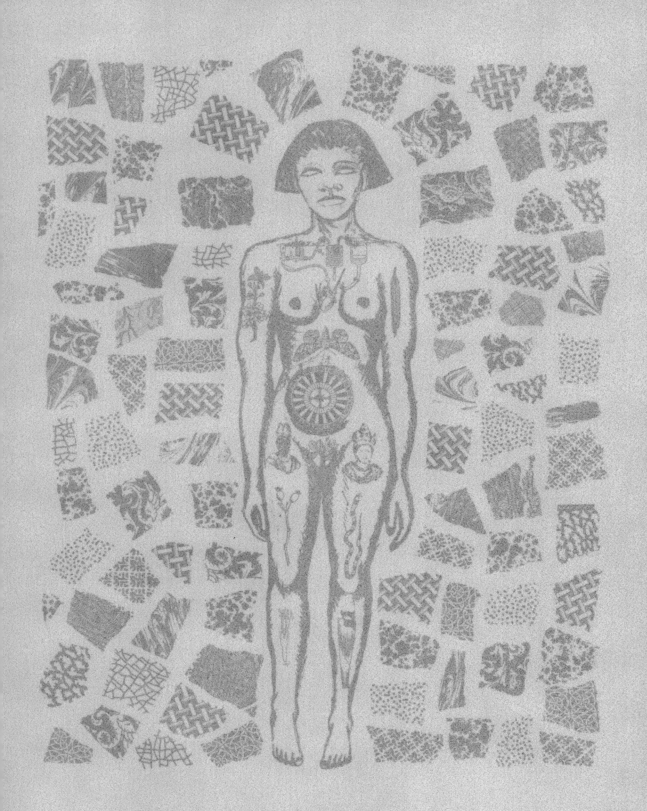

after Baudelaire's "The Muse for Hire"

Oh confused and demon heart
that mounts and pilfers hours;
the calendars are clogged too.
The years have 13 months each,
while January to January parades
lashed to the inevitable
in winter's anonymous darkness.

The hours are noiseless, the sores insensible,
the tissues of connection reel
as if in rented tuxedos,
droopy-eyed, a drunken brush away from violence.

Rein them in tight.
Don't trouble what doesn't break.
Don't violate the sense of purse or secondhand pleasure
recalled or lamented
that ring of truth and other
undetonated hazards.

How beautiful the reasonable grip of stock behavior
like an infant who leans and chants grasping
the cross of her crib
and springs tedium from the trap
but cannot escape herself.

Or sitting back, joins
eating to appetite
her laugh to pleasures
administered in low voltages
or her faith to the efficient
reduction of riddle.

Risk Signature

She likes to organize with her bare teeth.
Walking the wire with her baskets between
full and empty, she erects
scaffolding for her critiques
then isolates her objects with a deft
twitch of the knife.

There is a high tech cool
efficiency in what she achieves
what she is willing to store —
       the whopping calculations of the mutest reality
       where assertion is an omnivorous open
       bracket…
              abstraction quantified and baked into muffins;
              She stores the accidental in the breach between shame
              and satisfaction, almost wordless demiseconds
              of emotional itch noted faster than the hurry to
              scratch it.

The entries list the blood counts,
pound in the head as warnings to the wary, little
deaths configured into road kill
specimens collected, dried snake
smashed turtle, white bird skull.

What about danger?

Danger is engaged
as much as possible.
Organization entails foresight.
She tries to see things coming.

Biographical Suite

1. Ecstasy

What have we to look forward to but old age
an unfolding of the flesh into some foreign package
whose stamps we barely recognize
whose worries are like lint we pick up from nowhere
the scar of it from no accident we can recall
but obtained in the dark, in the dark
theater we embrace a faded script.

I can't explain it. I looked up from the page and
found myself fully grown.
It lasted for about an hour.

Here's my strength — to follow the meaning
even as it stands zig zag along the sheer edges
of sight; the brittle garlands of thought
jagged-toothed scaling the horizon.

Noted for my level head
even among these unfinished songs.
Instead of planning beauty, I, as they say
"let it happen." Let eyes connect the dots.
Air connive with the invisible.

Ecstasy is blind and moves on wings, torn feathers.

2. Shadow Box

Situation reversed, my father dies when he is young. Not me. He dies a boy, though he died my parent, a middle-aged man. The boy dies only a few days ago, I am told. The boy dies in me.

He is a young man of uncertain prospects and ambition. What dies? The boy dies because he is careless. Because of something he forgets to do. Was that his first death?

My father dies a young man, just a few days ago, tragically. I've done all my growing up without him. He meanwhile has stayed the same, the same age. He has never changed.

My father died young, out of season. Just as the good are said to die young. I am middle-aged, a woman of strong appetites and desires, furiously alive; a woman with a tongue in her head. At my age, I no longer live under virtue's shadow. Now I have only myself to praise or blame.

Did he run or was he chased? What raced with him to that final spot, shattering in white retinal glare? That young man in me, the other one who grieves?

When I was younger he never spoke so directly.

When he was younger I never spoke so directly.

Do moths know heaven drawn to a flame?

My father died young and I was surprised. I thought all these years had buried him, that maybe I'd outgrown him, redeemed him, knowing what I know, twice the woman, woman to the boy.

3. City of Heaven

I take pains to letter the streets. Grid made rigorous in all directions. Sky locked. Exits clearly marked. Lines ruled. Feet pointing the right way, never up. Streets crossed. Traffic light. Statues armed or at least labeled. Populace populous. Decorous youth prowling in grief-stricken black. Middle-aged adults utterly filled to the brim and thus of no use to anyone. Floorwalkers guarded. Streetwalkers spectacular. Police menacing or impossible to find. Parks geometric and park walker numbers rise exponential to the day's heat peaking at full noon. Radios rocket. Managers on ladders fight their descent on the food chain. Everyone else cut off, cut out to fit or lose.

In the long run, there is no such thing as balance. You are all the way in or you are out of bounds. There is no way to extinguish this dialectic except through draft after draft of textual ethics, the mechanics and clanking machinery of reader-focused phonetics. I feel transparent. As fast as light. Paradise, where there are innumerable back doors, and nothing to be afraid of. Nothing broken. Nothing fixed about it. Clarity in a blink of an eye.

Variation

During the day when everything distant falls in place

I

the sun (a marble spinning on a plate)
the sky (black plane of n dimensions)
consciousness (a room in which every detail fits,
    though can't necessarily be found)

words (worlds)
fury (gushes, an open wound)
joy (unwinds, changes shape)
each raising bodies from the text.

The apostrophe *behind* the noun.

II

    the speaker stands
    in front of shades of gray
    (a moment's notice)
    filling an empty page (a spotless room)
    with absolutes.

III

Only books contain streets
as serenely freighted as a
snapshot, a picture worth a thousand words,
for every hour of the day,
framed around a disinterested person
(the photographer forgets the image until
the figure fills the blank).

IV

The stack contains shortcuts (straight lines for visibility)
that join the known world (a shrinking list)
      one street connects another (borders are temporary)
        in cities chained by alphabet and accident
to everything that awaits a name.

COLLABORATIVE STATEMENT

Anymore than the world is flat…no blind dates just research mediated by a blow on the dice. We have this in common: art and life, children, daughters named Maddy, indefatigable acrobatic capacity to surf multiple projects from zero to upheaval.

Paper, scissors, stone…two years of exchange, short, long, short lengths of sun, strips of fog, show and tell leads to drafts and drafts jiggle pictures, pictures snap back, flames curl figures of speech, shapes recall shadows, shadows box.

Bends in the road…domestic sprawl, spectacle and opacity, calculated innocence and cruelty, social flamboyance and boundary, voices in the head, objects on the road, tact.

Erica Hunt/Alison Saar
March 1996

Arcade is a limited edition of two thousand copies;
fifty are numbered, and signed by the author,
and include an original, signed woodcut.

The text face is Optima; text film by Access Typography.
Halftones created by West Coast Print Center.
Design and typesetting by Poulson/Gluck.

Printed at West Coast Print Center on
Carnival Softwhite and Vellum UV II.

Kelsey St. Press   1996